"Photographs are fragile paper timeships,
dusted with information."

Joel Meyerowitz

DIANE ARBUS. *Identical Twins, Roselle, N.J.*, 1967. Courtesy Robert Miller Gallery, New York.
Copyright © Estate of Diane Arbus 1971.

COME
LOOK WITH ME

Discovering Photographs
With Children

Jean S. Tucker

THOMASSON-GRANT
Charlottesville, Virginia

For Zachary, Jed, Alexander and Thomas

ACKNOWLEDGMENTS

Several friends and colleagues have been supportive and helpful in the realization of this book. Special thanks are owed to Ann Morris, American Historian, Associate Director of the University Archives and Manuscript Collections, University of Missouri-St. Louis; Sara Jenkins, Art Historian and Editor; Rebecca Beall Barns, Editor, Thomasson-Grant; and Isabel Baker, The Book Vine for Children, McHenry, Illinois, for their guidance. Valuable assistance has come from the following photographic curators: Colin Westerbeck, Jr., The Art Institute of Chicago; Jeff Rosenheim, The Metropolitan Museum of Art; Olivia Gonzalez, The St. Louis Art Museum; and Virginia Dodier, The Museum of Modern Art. The galleries, museums, and individual photographers who have kindly given permission for the photographs to be published are here gratefully acknowledged.

In particular, I express my gratitude to Professor Lance LeLoup, Director of the Public Policy Research Centers at the University of Missouri-St. Louis, who has provided the office and support for my research since I retired from teaching.

Published by Thomasson-Grant, Inc.
Copyright © 1994 Thomasson-Grant, Inc.
Text © 1994 Jean S. Tucker
Edited by Rebecca Beall Barns

00 99 98 97 96 95 94   5 4 3 2 1

Any inquiries should be directed to Thomasson-Grant, Inc.
One Morton Drive, Suite 500
Charlottesville, Virginia 22903-6806
804 977-1780

Library of Congress Cataloging-in-Publication Data

Tucker, Jean S.
    Come look with me : discovering photographs with children /
Jean S. Tucker.
        p.   cm.
    ISBN 1-56566-062-5
    1. Photography of children — Juvenile literature. 2. Photography,
Artistic — Juvenile literature. 3. Photography — Study and teaching
(Elementary) [1. Photography, Artistic. 2. Art appreciation.]
    I. Title. II. Title: Discovering photographs with children.
    TR681.C5T83 1994
    770' . 1 — dc20   94 - 10835
                                                              CIP
                                                              AC

THOMASSON-GRANT

Contents

Preface

If you think that more pictures are taken of children than of any other subject, you are right. Parents take pictures of their children from birth through every happy occasion in childhood, until the children themselves begin to take their own photographs of the family.

Have you ever thought about the qualities that make the best pictures? Or do you simply have favorites without knowing exactly why? By looking carefully at the photographs of children in this book, we can begin to learn what makes a photograph special.

These pictures were taken by professional photographers—men and women who work every day to capture and preserve exceptional moments on film. Some of their images are lighthearted and sentimental, but some of them show a more somber side of life not usually seen in family albums. These photographs tell us much about the time and place in which they were taken if we are able to "read" them, for knowledge comes to us through pictures as powerfully as it does through words.

By looking slowly and thoughtfully at photographs, we may be able to see all that the photographer meant for us to see. Once you see it too, you will sense the magic that is in the picture.

Why do I say it is magic? Because a photograph, while looking like the subject, is not the same thing as the subject. It is at once a likeness and an interpretation. It has been made by a keen observer who gives us both a mirror image of what he or she has seen and a window through which we see the world.

Think of these ideas about photography as you enjoy the marvelous pictures of children in this book.

How to use this book

COME LOOK WITH ME: Discovering Photographs With Children is the fifth in the highly acclaimed COME LOOK WITH ME series of books for youngsters. Like the first four books on art appreciation for boys and girls, this one is to share with children, either with one child at a time or with a small group.

A set of open-ended questions accompanies each photograph, as does some background information on both the work and the photographer. The background information can be read silently, read aloud, or simply paraphrased while the book is open to the picture. Encourage each child to point to parts of the photograph while he or she talks about it. If you are sharing with a group, always ask if anyone has a different opinion. Our perceptions of photographs can be as different as we are as individuals—so many responses are possible, and few could really be considered wrong.

The pictures included here are by photographers whose work can be seen in books and in museums and galleries across the United States. Through this book and through visits to museums and galleries to see original works, children and adults will be inspired to share their observations and insights.

MATHEW BRADY STUDIO. *Henry James, Sr., and Henry James, Jr.*, 1854.
bMS. Am 1092.9 (4597) By permission of the Houghton Library, Harvard University.

What kinds of clues tell you that this is an old photograph?

Describe how this picture looks different from photographs of you with your parents.

Have you ever seen a photograph like this one close-up or held one in your hands? Ask your grandparents whether they have any old photographs of your relatives, and if they do, have them tell you as much as they can about the pictures and the people in them.

In the early days of photography, portraits were made in a very different way from the way they are made today. Portrait sessions, called "sittings," were planned and formal, and the people in them usually dressed in their finest clothes. They had to remain very still in front of the camera for much longer than the split second photographs take today. In most early portraits, like this one, the subjects look stiff and straight, and their faces are very serious.

This picture is called a daguerreotype. It was processed on a surface of highly polished silver, framed in gold, and protected in a special hinged case. The noted American writer Henry James and his father had this daguerreotype taken as a surprise gift for the boy's mother.

Henry James, Sr., sits on a chair and leans on his heavy cane, while his 12-year-old son stands by his side. To make sure that the boy stood still, the photographer supported his neck with a brace that is hidden from view. Unlike children today, who might pose with their arms around their father in a playful, affectionate way, the boy places his hand on his father's shoulder to show respect and devotion.

As a grown-up, young Henry treasured this photograph. He proudly wrote that the picture proved how much his father wanted to be with him.

CLARENCE HUDSON WHITE. *Ring Toss*, 1899.
Courtesy of the Library of Congress.

There are many contrasts in this picture. Can you find some (light and dark, near and far, motion and stillness)?

Would you like to join in this game? Why or why not? Contrast this game to the way girls play today.

Clarence White started out as a painter, but his parents didn't approve of painting as a career or even as a hobby, so at the age of 23, White began to teach himself how to take photographs. This quiet scene of a game of ring toss is typical of what he liked to photograph—young girls in a domestic setting bathed in soft, natural light.

The details in this photograph are softened by the quality of light and by the placement of the figures deep into the picture space. The photographer carefully arranged the figures—where they are in the room and how they relate to each other. He even designed the dresses the girls are wearing.

White's thoughtful manipulation of light and the tones of dark and light in his pictures gave his work a distinctive, luminous quality. He sometimes enhanced his photographs by marking on them with pencil or white ink. In this picture, he added lines along the left arm and shoulder of the girl tossing the ring to make her stand out against the background. Since the invention of photography, some artists have altered their images to achieve a number of different effects.

RUTH ORKIN. *Jimmy, The Storyteller, Greenwich Village, New York*, 1946.
© 1994 Estate of Ruth Orkin.

Do you think Jimmy's friends are interested in his story? What do you see in the photograph that makes you think that?

Hands can play an important role in storytelling. What is Jimmy doing with his?

This photograph is an image from a six-part picture story. Like a single frame from a motion picture, it captures an instant in a storyteller's tale and the audience's reaction. The photographer's ability to convey an important part of Jimmy's story in this picture is related to her skills in movie-making.

Ruth Orkin wanted to be a filmmaker, but in her day, professional film organizations did not accept women, so she became a photojournalist, someone who works quickly to take pictures of stories as they happen. She began her career in the 1940s with assignments from major magazines including *Life, Colliers,* and *Ladies' Home Journal.*

Orkin must have been very near these children when she took their picture, but she managed to work without calling attention to herself. The boys seem to be relaxed and comfortable in her presence. By looking carefully at each part of the picture, at the hands, expressions, and gestures, we see the details that bring the scene to life. The boy on the right, for instance, plunked his hat down on his head hard enough to mash his ear!

Ruth Orkin's mother noted that as a child, her observant daughter was always pointing things out to her. "Look at this! Look at that!" she would say. Taking photographs was her way of getting people to look more carefully at the world around them.

BARBARA MORGAN. *Children Singing in the Rain*, 1950.
Barbara and Willard Morgan Archives © 1980.

Even though it is a rainy day, light sparkles across this picture. Point to the areas where you see the most light.

If you could step into this picture, describe the sounds you would hear, the taste of rain on your tongue, and how the rain would feel on your skin. Have you ever caught raindrops in your mouth?

The word photograph means "writing with light." Barbara Morgan was one of the leading photographers whose pictures were about light and movement in light. She made a series of photographs called "light draw-ings" for which she strapped a flashlight to her wrist and photographed the patterns made by the light in a dark room. "Photography would not exist without light," she said, "and neither would life."

As a child growing up in California, Barbara Morgan liked to watch raindrops fall from the slender leaves of a eucalyptus tree outside her house. "After the sun came out," she said, "I would sit enthralled watching the light center in each tiny raindrop—filled with secret mystery!"

In the 1950s, Barbara Morgan took many photographs of her children and their friends at a summer camp in the Adirondack Mountains of New York. At Camp Treetops, the children grew their own food and lived close to nature. Morgan photographed campers dancing, jumping, playing musi-cal instruments—and singing in the rain.

In this photograph, Morgan conveys the children's delight as they catch raindrops in their open mouths. Like little flowers, their faces reach up for light and water. Morgan's ability to capture light and shadow can be seen in the contrast between the light in the clearing and the darkness of the trees that border it.

ALFRED EISENSTAEDT. *Drum Major and Children, University of Michigan,* 1951.
Life Magazine, © Time Warner Inc.

What do you see in the photograph that gives the feeling of open space?

What made the children want to follow the drum major?

Do you think the drum major knows the children are behind him? What makes you think that?

In 1951, *Life* Magazine photographer Alfred Eisenstaedt was assigned a picture story on the University of Michigan's marching band. He took all of the usual kinds of photographs of people marching in formation and rehearsing. One day, while he was walking across the campus, he came upon a drum major practicing his strutting. A group of children playing nearby soon fell in behind him, mimicking his high step.

Because it happened so quickly, Eisenstaedt didn't have time to bring the picture into sharp focus. "If you're there—and react fast enough—it's okay," he said, regarding the fact that the picture isn't absolutely sharp. The photographer's response to what he or she sees makes all the difference. Perhaps the reason this photograph is so memorable is that it expresses so well the excitement Eisenstaedt felt when he captured the moment on film.

Eisenstaedt's photographs appeared in more than 1,000 picture stories in *Life* Magazine over the course of 40 years. His work was also selected for the most well-known photographic exhibit ever—The Family of Man—which opened at The Museum of Modern Art in 1955.

DIANE ARBUS. *Identical Twins, Roselle, N.J.*, 1967. Courtesy Robert Miller Gallery, New York.
Copyright © Estate of Diane Arbus 1971.

Even though these sisters look very much alike, they differ in certain ways. Can you see any? If so, what are they?

Do their clothes make it easier or more difficult to see the differences?

Do you know any identical twins? If so, take their picture and discover the differences between them. If not, take pictures of your brothers and sisters or your parents and try to find features that are alike and some that are different.

At first glance, this photograph seems so simple. There seems to be no action or story, and yet we look and look and look at these sisters, searching for the slightest differences. There are two of everything—headbands, bobbie pins, dresses, pairs of stockings, pairs of hands. Our eyes move back and forth from one twin to the other to compare their eyes, their mouths, and the way each one stands, looking for details that help distinguish each girl from the other.

The main focus of Diane Arbus's work was people. She rarely took pictures of any other subject. She placed the people in the center and very close to the foreground of the picture, which is called the picture plane. This brings the viewer close to the twins in this photograph and makes us relate to them in a more direct way. With her keen eye and distinctive style, Arbus shows us small but important things that we might otherwise miss. "I really believe," she once said, "there are things which no one would see unless I photographed them."

Diane Arbus dared to take pictures of people who are different—dwarfs, the mentally ill, some we think should be pitied. She believed that everyone is important and that everyone is exceptional in some way. Her photographs help teach us to look at people with more care and to respect them as individuals.

HELEN LEVITT. *Untitled,* 1972.
© Helen Levitt 1994.

What kind of neighborhood are these children playing in?
What details in the picture tell you that?

Compare this photograph to the portrait of Henry James
and his son. How are children portrayed differently in the two
pictures?

Helen Levitt was one of the first photographers in the United States
to become known for "street photography." By the 1940s, when she began
photographing children in the streets of New York, the invention of a
small, hand-held camera and improvements in film had made it possible
to take action photographs quickly and easily without being noticed.

Levitt began making color photographs in 1959. She took this one in
1972 in the East Village in New York City as she passed by these children
playing with a laundry cart. Like a frame from a homemade movie, this
scene gives us a real look at children at play, unaware of the photographer's
presence. The careful though informal composition gives the observer a
cut-off view and a feeling of immediacy.

Unlike a painter, who can choose the colors he or she will work with,
a photographer capturing an action scene on color film must work with the
color that is already there. The browns, blacks, reds, and yellows on the
walls in the background are repeated in the children's clothing. This helps
lead our eyes around the photograph from one child to another and back
again to take in all the details, to wonder what the children are saying to
each other and what they are seeing, as if we, too, had chanced upon them
in the street.

JOEL MEYEROWITZ. *Chuckie, 1981.*
© Joel Meyerowitz 1994.

What are some of the details in the picture that tell you it is summertime?

What happened to Chuckie's neck?

Why do you think Chuckie is carrying the fish that way?

This picture is one from a series of photographs made by Joel Meyerowitz during seven summers he spent in Cape Cod. Each image takes him back to the exact moment he made it and reminds him of his favorite time of year. Through his vivid color photographs, Meyerowitz evokes the joys of summer: the warmth and glow of summer light, the freedom and contentment that come when days are long and people can be outside in lighter clothing.

Meyerowitz made this photograph with a large camera, an 8 x 10 viewfinder. He looks through the viewfinder to compose the image, steps to the side, and asks his subject to look directly into the camera. He talks to the person until he sees an expression he wants, then takes the picture. Most of the time, he captures a more serious look with this kind of camera than he does with a small, hand-held one.

The photographer was taking pictures of other people on the dock when he saw Chuckie walk by wearing an old, spattered windbreaker and carrying a great bluefish on his shoulders. When Meyerowitz asked him to stop so he could take his photograph, the boy agreed, looking intently into the camera lens.

TOM ARNDT. *Ballerinas, Bud Bilikin Day Parade, Chicago.* 1987.
© Tom Arndt 1994. Art Institute of Chicago, gift of the Focus/Infinity Fund, 1988.

Ballerinas usually perform on a stage. How can you tell that these dancers are out of doors?

Look carefully at how the girls are standing. What does it say about how they are feeling?

What do you suppose the girl in the center sees outside the picture frame?

Tom Arndt has been documenting life on the streets of Chicago since he moved there in 1989. To learn as much as he can about the city, he walks the streets, rides buses and trains, and attends the same public celebrations each year, documenting what he sees with a camera. Though his photographs are of Chicago, they reveal a great deal about life in large American cities.

Each August, Arndt attends the Bud Bilikin Day Parade, a 40-year-old tradition in honor of a well-known Black comicstrip character featured in the *Chicago Defender*, a newspaper from South Chicago. The parade, which takes place on Martin Luther King Drive in South Chicago, is a big community celebration, a time for families and friends to gather and talk and have a good time.

The ballerinas in this picture are getting ready to take part in the parade. The figures in the background and to the right are cut off at the edge of the photograph, giving the viewer the feeling of being in a crowd. By showing only a part of the face of the girl on the right, the photographer encourages us to extend the picture in space, to look beyond. The photograph gives an idea of what it's like to be in a parade—the gesturing, talking, waiting, and being in the center of all the excitement.

NANCY ACKERMAN. *Silas Quluat, Inuit near Igloolik*, 1991.
© Nancy Ackerman 1994.

Why do you think the photographer composed the picture with the boy to one side instead of in the center?

Can you imagine this photograph in black and white? What important details would you lose?

Compare this photograph to the one of Chuckie and the fish.

This picture is of Silas Quluat, a young Inuit boy who lives in the Canadian Arctic. He plays with other children in a camp along the Arctic Ocean while waiting for his father to return from a walrus hunt. For hours at a time, he and his friends play games in the ice and snow.

It is three o'clock in the morning, and Silas and his friends aren't even thinking about sleep. They live in the Land of the Midnight Sun, where in the summertime the sun barely sets. Silas spends most of his time outside, and his nose runs from constant exposure to the wind and cold.

This image nearly sings with the exhilaration of being out in the early morning in the clear, cold air. The fur on the boy's hood blows in a brisk wind. In the background, an expanse of ice and bright blue northern sky stretches as far as the eye can see.

The photographer, Nancy Ackerman, spent five days in the fishing camp while taking photographs of Silas's relatives for a project on Native American women. Of Mohawk Indian descent, Ackerman brings a keen interest and sensitivity to her coverage of Native Americans.

DENNIS BRACK. *The Dancers, National Gallery of Art, Washington, D.C.*, 1992.
© Dennis Brack/Black Star.

28

Why do you think the girl stopped and posed like the dancers?

Have you ever posed to look like someone in a work of art you've seen?

Why do you think people go to art museums?

In 1991, the National Gallery of Art in Washington, D.C., hired Dennis Brack to take pictures for a special book to celebrate the gallery's 50th anniversary. His assignment was to show that the gallery is not just a building where people file by great works of art, but an exciting place where visitors learn about art, respond to it, and most of all, enjoy it.

In this photograph, a young girl strikes a pose inspired by George Segal's sculpture of dancers. It's easy to imagine that she was probably not the first, nor the last, to respond to the sculpture this way. In what is called "the decisive moment," Brack brought the key elements—light, composition, movement, and meaning—together to make a timeless photograph.

Since the early 1970s, Dennis Brack has photographed people and events in Washington, D.C., for magazines throughout the world. A noted political photographer, he has covered the White House for years and has travelled with several presidents on trips to foreign countries.

The year he worked on the book for the National Gallery, Brack made three trips to the Middle East to cover the Gulf War. Images of war were very much on his mind when he returned to take photographs in the gallery. It must have been a poignant moment when he captured this young girl in such a serene and graceful pose.

MICHAEL NICHOLS. *Cupid, the Hippo*, 1993.
© Michael Nichols/Magnum.

Sunlight shines through the water from above. What kind of mood does this create in the photograph?

What do you suppose the boy is thinking about? Why don't you need to see his face to guess?

Does the photograph make you want to visit a zoo? Why or why not?

Michael Nichols cares very much about the protection of the world's living creatures and their natural environment and has made this a focus of his work. For a decade he has photographed natural history topics, including the great apes: orangutans, chimpanzees, and gorillas.

Nichols took this photograph at the Toledo Zoo Hippoquarium while working on an article on zoos for *National Geographic* Magazine. Zoo officials had suggested that he come at a quiet time so that he could take the best photographs of the animals, but Nichols wanted crowds, too. He was looking for the kind of encounter between animals and humans that would remind people of why zoos exist. So one Sunday, from opening to closing time, he stood by the underground exhibit and took more than 1,000 photographs as people walked by. In this image, a peaceful scene in the midst of the zoo's most popular exhibit, a young boy gently brushes the glass as Cupid the Hippo swims gracefully alongside him.

Of thousands of pictures the photographer submitted to *National Geographic* for the article on zoos, photo editors could choose just 29 to tell the story. Of those, the photographer considers this one his best.

Selected Bibliography

An Aperture Monograph. *diane arbus.* New York: The Museum of
   Modern Art, 1972.

Eisenstaedt, Alfred, and Goldsmith, Arthur. *the eye of Eisenstaedt.* New York:
   Viking Press, 1969.

Gattuso, John, Ed. *A Circle of Nations: Voices and Visions of American Indians.*
   Hillsboro, Oregon: Beyond Words Publishing, Inc., 1993.

Kismaric, Susan. *American Children.* New York: The Museum of
   Modern Art, 1980.

Meyerowitz, Joel. *A Summer's Day.* New York: Time Books, 1985.

Newhall, Beaumont. *The History of Photography from 1839 to the Present.*
   New York: The Museum of Modern Art, 1982 ed.

Orkin, Ruth. *A Photo Journal.* New York: The Viking Press, 1981.

Pfister, Harold. *Facing the Light: Historic American Portrait Daguerreotypes.*
   Washington, D.C.: Smithsonian Institution Press, 1978.

Rosenblum, Naomi. *A World History of Photography.* New York: Abbeville
   Press, 1984.

Steichen, Edward. *The Family of Man.* New York: The Museum of
   Modern Art, 1955.

Szarkowski, John. *Mirrors and Windows: American Photography Since 1960.*
   New York: The Museum of Modern Art, 1978.

Time-Life Books. *Photographing Children.* New York: Time-Life Books, 1971.